Enjoy.

Thanks for drinking responsibly.

www.beeresponsible.com

10 Places Where Money Is Hidden In Your Restaurant

& *how to find it!*

Go for it

Bill Quain

By Bill Quain, Ph.D.

Published by Wales Publishing Company
North Wales, PA

Printed in the United States

ISBN 0-9623646-2-2

Table Of Contents

About The Author

Bill Quain, Ph.D. (www.quain.com) is a professor at Florida International University's famed School of Hospitality Management. He is a well-known consultant, speaker and author, having written nine books on marketing, personal growth and profit generation. Bill is also the author of numerous articles, including a highly acclaimed, four-part series on revenue enhancement for the Cornell Hotel and Restaurant Administration Quarterly.

Bill's books and articles are for people with work to do. Using plain language and proven strategies, he provides practical solutions for people who want to accomplish specific goals - primarily, MAKING MORE MONEY!

Dr. Quain is a graduate of Cornell University, Florida International University and the University of New Orleans. He has been a professor, consultant, writer and speaker for over 20 years, in a variety of industries. Before joining the ranks of academia, Bill was a hotel and restaurant owner/operator. Over the course of his career, he has developed a keen sense of where the money is hidden. Now, he shares that information with you.

Other books by Bill Quain, Ph.D.:

Selling Your Services to the Meetings Market
The Marketing Plan Project Manual
Reclaiming The American Dream: The Keys To Financial Freedom
10 Rules To Break & 10 Rules To Make: The Do's and Don'ts For
    Designing Your Destiny

And coming soon, more books in the 10 Places Where Money Is Hidden series, including money-making, customer-satisfying books like:

10 Places Where Money Is Hidden In Your...

...Hotel
...Catering Company
...Association
...Convention
...Special Event
...Club

...Sports Tournament
...Medical Practice
...Dental Practice
...Rental Business

Bill is looking for co-authors in various fields and industries to create new versions of 10 Places Where Money Is Hidden. If you are interested in co-authoring a book with Bill, or if you have an idea for a new version of the book, please contact him at (305) 944-7673. You can also send an e-mail to bill@quain.com.

Acknowledgments And Dedication

The author would like to thank the following people and organizations for their help in compiling this book:

Darrell Wilde for ideas, input, creative suggestions and great examples of customer-satisfying restaurant operations

Joel Williams for getting the idea into production

The Florida Restaurant Association for their vision and support

Jeanne Quain, my wife, for her patient editing and rewrites

Catherine Quain, my mother, for her help with the editing

Beth Nibert, Craig Brockman, and Jeff and Athena Staton from Staton Publications, who did the layout and design

And finally, the editors of the Cornell Quarterly for their assistance in shaping these ideas

This book is dedicated to my daughters, Amanda and Kathleen Quain. Through their innocent eyes, I learn creativity all over again.

Introduction

This is a book about making more money. That sounds very simple. But for too many people, the prospect of increasing the rewards for their work is complicated by one strong emotion - fear. Believe it or not, too many people are afraid that they will upset their customers by generating more income for themselves. Nothing could be further from the truth!

The only way to make more money is to satisfy the needs of customers and clients BETTER than anyone else can do it! The only way to get customers to spend more money is to make them happier! The only way to increase profits is to develop strong, long-term relationships with people who are depending on YOU to give them what they want. That is how money is made! And that is what this book is designed to teach you how to do.

This book will show you 10 places to immediately look for hidden money in your business. Of course, it would be impossible for me to outline ALL of the places where money is hidden. But, by reading this book, you will learn how to keep on finding more hidden money. In fact, you will be in the position to create more satisfied customers, and hence, more money, continuously, FOR THE REST OF YOUR CAREER!

How can this be possible? Well, like making more money, it is simple. Just remember the old saying, "Give a man a fish and he will eat for a day, but TEACH A MAN TO FISH and he will feed his family for a lifetime." That is what this book is designed to do. Yes, you will benefit now from the last chapter - the one with 10 places where money is hidden. However, the greatest treasure is in the first five chapters. In these chapters, you will discover the secrets to creating satisfied customers by giving them more of what they want. You will learn to use creativity and innovation to reinvent your business. You will learn "how to fish".

It is up to you. Are you ready to start fishing?

Chapter 1
Creating More Wealth
In Your Current Business
Sponsored By

Wealth creation, or revenue enhancement, is simply *getting more income from a limited resource.* All businesses have at least two limited resources - time and money. You *cannot* create more time, but you *can* make more money. This book is about doing just that - creating more money - by doing the things you are already doing.

The airlines call this process "yield management". They have airplanes. The planes have seats that need to be filled. And in order for the airlines to create more revenue, they must make more money every time a seat is sold.

Did you ever see a discounted flight advertised on television or in the newspaper? Were you EVER able to book it? Probably not. By the time you contacted the airline, those seats were already sold. Sure, you could have booked a seat at the NEXT price. There were plenty of <u>those</u> seats.

Why? Because the airlines have made a lifelong study of how to get the *very most revenue* from *limited resources*. And, they are very successful at it!

What about your business? Are you maximizing your revenues? Are you serving only the <u>best</u> customers, and making every dime you can on <u>each</u> transaction? Have you even CONSIDERED that more money might be out there, right under your very nose? It is there, you know. But you need a plan, a system, just like the airlines. You have to WANT that money in order to get it.

It doesn't matter what kind of business you own. There is probably <u>more</u> money in it for you. Whether you are an owner or an employee, there are ways to maximize the yield in your business. **Ten** of those methods are discussed in the following pages.

But this book is much more than just a list of places to find money. After all, how much help would it be just to give you a few clues? By reading this book, and implementing some of the suggestions, you can embark on a whole PROGRAM of increasing wealth. You will learn how to sustain the impact of your new enthusiasm to CONTINUE making more money - permanently!

There is an old saying: "Give a man a fish and he will have a meal. Teach a man HOW to fish and he can feed himself forever." This book is designed to teach you how to fish - for hidden revenue!

Yield Management

There is a classic story that illustrates just how easy it is to make more money through yield management. J.W.(Bill) Marriott was the owner of the famous chain of hotels that bears his name. In the early days, however, the family only had one hotel. This hotel had a drive-up window where guests would pull in to pay for a room. The Marriotts charged a flat fee for the room, and $1 extra per guest if there was more than one person staying overnight. On nights when the motel was almost full, Mr. Marriott would lean out the window of the registration area and look down the line of cars waiting to get a room.

If the next car in line only had one passenger, Mr. Marriott would not sell the potential customer a room. He would save the rooms for groups of two or three. By selling them the rooms, he made a little extra each time.

You may be thinking, "He only made a dollar or two more per room. That isn't much. I was hoping this book would show me how to make LOTS more money."

Let me say two things. First, in those days, a dollar <u>was</u> a lot of money. Second, are you making a fortune each time you serve a customer right now? If you have one customer, do you charge them so much that you can retire after they pay their bill? Of course not. Revenue and yield management are the same way.

You should be looking for ways to make SMALL amounts of money each time you serve another customer. If you are consistent, persistent, and GOOD, those small increases will add up VERY, VERY, QUICKLY. You will make a lot more money by simply doing the things you are already doing, but doing them better.

A Story Of Success

Two men were sitting in a sports bar, watching the Tour de France on television. (The Tour is a grueling, three-week bicycle race that covers over two thousand miles of mountains, valleys, and city streets in France each year. It is a brutal event, where the riders battle each other, often in inclement weather.)

"I don't understand why anyone would put themselves through that ordeal," said the first man.

"Why?" asked his friend.

"Why?!? Those riders have to struggle up incredible mountains, racing back down at break-neck speeds. They race in the hot sun, driving rain, fog, and sometimes even snow, for three weeks. It is a terrible thing!"

"The winner gets millions of dollars in endorsements and other prizes," said the friend.

"Oh, I understand why the WINNER does it," said the man. "But why would all those OTHER guys do it?"

He has a good point. Why would all those other guys do it? Why would YOU do what YOU do? You know why - for the rewards!

Are You A Winner, Or Just A RACER?

Every industry, every occupation or profession, is a race. Some races are fun, others are not. But, in all cases, they have rewards that may, or may not, make the race worth it. What kind of race are you in?

Your answer is probably "The RAT Race".

It sure seems that way. These days, everyone is rushing around, trying to balance work and personal time, looking for the rewards which our professions can bring. Too many people are satisfied just to be in the race. But it isn't the race that provides the rewards. It is the man or woman who not only puts forth the effort, but also has the right strategy, who will reap the great rewards. The others, the people who simply participate, can pick up some honors here and there. They might even make a LIVING at it. But, it is the WINNER who will look back on the race and know that it was all worth it. The others will only have memories of the struggle.

Winning: A Team Concept

For too many people, the thought of winning something is very scary. They assume that in order to win, they need to beat everyone else. That may be true for sports events like the Tour de France, but happily it is not the case in business. In business, there can be many, many winners. You don't have to beat everyone else. Winners create rewards that GROW as more and more people win.

Stephan Covey, the world famous author of *Seven Habits of Highly Effective People,* has discovered there are two kinds of attitudes: an attitude of ABUNDANCE, and an attitude of SCARCITY. There is a great deal of difference between these two ways of thinking. People who believe in scarcity assume that there is only so much of something. In other words, they believe that if one person wins, everyone else loses. However, people who believe in abundance realize there is <u>plenty</u> to go around. And, abundance-believers know that the more we create and innovate, the more opportunities there will be for EVERYONE.

Be an "abundance" personality. There <u>is</u> plenty for everyone. ANYONE can achieve greater potential.

There are so many rewards in your business, that you can create a TEAM of winners, and still have plenty for everyone. So, when you think of winning, don't imagine yourself beating out everyone else - including your own team. Imagine INCREASING THE REWARDS, so everyone can win.

Why Don't People Make More Money?

There are six main reasons why people do not realize all the profits from their businesses. This applies to both the employees and the owners of these businesses. The good news is, each of these challenges can be overcome. It is simply a matter of having a new perspective, a solid goal, and a vision of the way your business could run. Consider the following factors that hold you back from the money hidden in your business:

1. **People are not taught to create wealth**. We are not taught to dig out profits, and to seize all the opportunities that are presented to us. Our educational system is simply not set up for it. We should be learning to identify customer needs, and to take every opportunity to make money from solving their problems. <u>That</u> is the secret to wealth.

Think about it. What did you learn in school? Did your professors teach you to MAKE MONEY? Probably not. Instead, most of us learned theories and "management practices". And how about the "on-the-job-training" you received? Was that designed to teach you to seek out opportunities, create and bundle new products and services, to add value for your customers - in exchange for money? Probably not. In truth, most of us have become "corporatized" - hidden safely in layer upon layer of overlapping corporate structure.

In order to make money and create wealth, you must do the things that most people are simply not trained to do. It is a whole different way of viewing the business you are in.

2. **Many people do not understand the needs of their customers or clients.** And this costs them money -lots of money! It is one of the big reasons that money is hiding in your business right now. The customer or client is the key to achieving greater wealth. After all, they are the only ones who will give you money.

Dog food companies are a great example of an industry that <u>does</u> understand the needs of their customers. They advertise products that are "meaty" or "make their own gravy". One company has developed a series of dog foods that are specifically designed for different stages in a dog's life. Another company specializes in single serving wrappers. Why is this so noteworthy? Because it is not the dogs who are buying this stuff. It is the owners. Have you ever seen a dog standing in line, trying to decide which brand is best for her growing family of puppies? NO! Dogs drink out of the toilet bowls! Why should they care if they have the same food two nights in a row? All they care about is surviving so they can chase the newspaper boy one more day.

<u>People</u> buy dog food. They will buy expensive dog food if they are given the opportunity. They <u>want</u> to spend money on their pets. It makes them feel good. If they buy dog food, they will also buy treats and snacks for their dogs too. Yes, dog food suppliers have gotten the spirit.

You see, this is the big secret. People WANT to spend money.

They don't want to save it. They want to use it for their benefit. When someone goes on vacation, do they come home and say "Wow, I had a great time. I left the house with $500 and I came home with $450. I only spent fifty bucks on my vacation. What a great time we had!" No, people WANT to spend money. Just give them the chance.

3. Making more money requires more effort. I would like to tell you otherwise, but I can not. It requires more effort to make more money. That is the simple truth.

In today's economy, it is relatively easy to make SOME money. This is a consumer society. Demand is high for almost everything. Take a restaurant for example. If you have a restaurant, and it is not busy on Friday and Saturday night, then you should close it and make it a parking lot. EVERYONE IS DINING OUT THESE DAYS. Resorts, retail stores, and professional offices are all experiencing strong demand. It is very difficult not to make SOME money.

Unfortunately, many people assume that there is no way to substantially increase the amount of money they are making. There is, but *it requires effort*. You have to work at it, consistently.

But here's the good news. In this book, you will learn how to work *smarter*, with *little more effort*, to achieve big rewards. It is pretty simple. All it takes is a little imagination, and a strong desire to achieve greater wealth.

4. People think they are not "smart" enough to make more money. Creating wealth is not brain surgery. (Well, that is, of course, unless you make a living as a brain surgeon.) It is usually just a simple matter of LOOKING for it. Have you ever really LOOKED FOR THE MONEY IN YOUR BUSINESS? I ask that question, because many people do not. They are perfectly willing to ACCEPT money, but they do not actually SEEK IT OUT.

 You don't have to be a mental giant to make money. Thank goodness for that! It is simply a matter of dedicating yourself to the search for it.

We had two dogs named Abercrombie and Fitch. Fitch was an

escape artist. She wouldn't run away. She would just escape from the back yard and go sit in the front yard. She did it nearly every day. I would come home from work and there she would be, waiting for me in the front yard just so pleased with herself. I would go out back and try to figure out how she escaped. Sometimes I found the route she took, other times I did not.

How did that little dog outsmart me? Simple. She had nothing else to think about - nothing else to do all day besides looking for a way to get out of the yard. I was only willing to spend a few minutes trying to prevent her from escaping. For her, it was a lifetime commitment!

Fitch did not do a lot of deep thinking. She just got creative. She was determined to get out. All you need is the same determination.

5. People are too busy "putting out fires". It is difficult to do long range planning, or even SHORT range planning, when things are going crazy at work. In fact, it is sometimes hard to do any kind of planning whatsoever. For most of us, the stress and pressures of all the things that are going wrong demand all our attention. Doesn't it always seem like the person you need the most is either sick, on vacation, or having a baby? And that's the male employees!

But, if you can find the time to increase your profits, you may be able to use that money to actually *prevent* the fires. In particular, using some of the extra money to create incentives will reduce turnover and absenteeism. It's like a giant snowball effect - except this one is a *cascade of cash!*

6. People overlook the fact that they can start earning more money right now! Think about it. You already have a business. There are already customers, suppliers, production and service capabilities. You have a license, the training is finished. So, all the up-front costs and delays have already been taken care of. You are ready to enhance your revenue RIGHT NOW.

This means that the next customer who walks through the door, or even the one who is in your place of business right now, can provide you with more money than the last one did. All you have to do is determine how you will go about it. Sure, some programs will take months to develop. However, in each type of business, there are things you can do IMMEDIATELY to start increasing revenue.

So, get with it. Start right now. And, start with the easy things first. As my friend Dennis Quinn would say *"Pick the low hanging fruit"*. Look for the quickest, easiest ways to find the money that is hidden all around you. Don't worry about the really hard stuff. You will have time for that later. Right now, put together a team and a plan. Create some small successes. Then, after your team has confidence, you can begin to attack the more complicated problems.

Too many people want to wait until everything is exactly right before they even start creating wealth. You will wait forever if this is your attitude. Most of the time, the only thing that is preventing you from at least making a START is some kind of fear. It may be a fear that you will annoy your customers. Or, you may wonder why your competition didn't think of it. "If they aren't doing it, how good could it be?" is a common statement. Just recognize this fact:

When you avoid taking action for some reason, that reason is undoubtedly some kind of fear. Get over it! You are just making an excuse. You are in business to make money, so go ahead and make it - lots of it. Don't let your fears hold you back.

Summary

You *can* make more money - right now! Read this book to discover at least <u>ten</u> ways to increase your revenue. You will never have wealth unless you create it. You have to earn it - one customer at a time.

Money Making Strategy #1
How Much *More* Money Do You Want To Make?

I know this is a little scary, but you must commit yourself to a goal. How much more money would you like to make in the next 90 days?   I know it's early in the book, and you haven't yet discovered just how many ways there are to make more money in your business. So pick a number - make it reasonable yet meaningful.

As you read the rest of this book, keep this number in mind. Whenever you come across a good wealth-creating idea, put it into perspective. Will it meet your goals?

In the next 90 days, I would like to generate _____.

(extra money)

Chapter 2
Choosing The Right Customer
Sponsored By

There is an excellent story about customer development from the famous Nordstrom's Department Store. (I must admit, I personally do not know if it is true or not. However, there are so many accounts of utterly outstanding customer service from this company that there must be SOME truth to most of them.)

A woman bought a pair of shoes at a competitor's store and took them home. She discovered they were too small and decided to take them back. However, she found herself near a Nordstrom's and decided to take the shoes into the store with her, to see if the department store had the exact same style, but in her preferred size.

11

Her plan was to buy the new shoes at Nordstrom's, then return the other shoes to the original store.

The sales clerk found the style and the correct size and fitted the customer. When the customer attempted to pay for the shoes, the clerk said, "Just give me the other pair and I will exchange it for the new ones." "But I didn't buy these shoes here," said the customer. "I understand that," said the sales clerk, "but, I don't want to give you an excuse to go back into that store. I will take them in exchange here, and then we may be able to keep you as a customer." Obviously, the sales clerk had identified a good customer. Have you identified your best customers? Are you giving them an excuse to spend their money somewhere else?

You do not want EVERYONE to be your customer. I know this may come as a shock to some of my readers. "What do you MEAN?", you may be thinking. "I want ANYONE who is willing to pay my price to be my customer. I can never have enough customers!"

Well, you may be right about never having enough customers. However, there are some people who are not right for your business. You do not want them as customers or clients, because they will cost you money in the long run. You want only the very best customers for your particular service or product.

Who Is The Right Customer?

The right customer is one that you can satisfy. He or she is the person who is going to give you money, and do it gladly. This is someone with a problem that you can solve. And, the right customer is the person who is so happy when you solve their problems that they will run out and tell other people, people just like them, that you can solve THEIR problems too.

You want customers with the following characteristics:

1. **The customer has a problem.** Remember, you are a problem-solver-for-hire. Your ideal customer NEEDS something, and KNOWS they need something. Look for people who have a problem, solve their problem, and charge them for it.

2. The customer wants you to stay in business - Your customers, that is, your GOOD customers, want you to make money. They NEED you to make money. If you are solving their problems, the last thing they want is for you to go out of business. Relax. These people are willing to pay you.

3. They are willing to spend - The best customers are those who have the money, and are willing to spend it right now. They will spend more than the average person does for your type of business. They will not complain about the price, nor will they worry about your profit margin. This is a great customer.

4. The customer is loyal - I once heard a salesman say that his favorite prospect was one who would <u>only</u> buy from the competition. The salesman admired the customer's loyalty. So, he would do EVERYTHING possible to win that customer over. He would try to get a SMALL piece of their business first, and after establishing a relationship, he would try to get a little more. He knew that a loyal customer was a valuable customer. He wanted them to be loyal to HIM.

5. They are frequent buyers - Your best customers will buy your product or service more frequently, and for different uses. For example, a restaurant client may bring business partners to lunch for a sales talk, his spouse in for a romantic dinner, and his friends in for birthday celebrations. He is a good customer, because he uses the service more than the average person.

6. This person is willing to spend more - They have no problem giving you more money. Just show them how to spend it! They are in your place of business because you are good at solving their problems.

Identify the right customers. Invite them to spend time with you. The more time they are exposed to your products and services, the more time they have to spend money - and the less time they will have to spend it with your competitors.

The Opportunity To Spend

Are your customers or clients getting every opportunity to spend their money? I was a consultant for a riverboat in New Orleans. It was a really terrific experience. We would cruise the Mississippi, watching the scenery on both land and water. The captain would point out areas of interest, such as the famous battlefields, Jackson Square, and even passing ships. But the travelers who sailed with us were not given enough opportunity, or information, to spend their money!

The "Texas Bar" on the riverboat was a great example. Did you know that the third deck on a steamboat is traditionally called the "Texas Deck"? If you didn't, you may have been one of our customers - they didn't know it either. And besides being a great bit of trivia to know, it also would have been an excellent clue as to the LOCATION OF THE "TEXAS BAR"! But since our customers were not given this information, the "Texas Bar" was vastly underutilized, even on busy cruises.

Our customers would sit on the <u>second</u> deck, (the one they entered on), enjoying the sights. They could have been enjoying a cool beverage upstairs, instead! We would have made more money, and they would have purchased even more vacation memories.

One of the simple tactics for making more money is to give your customers the opportunity to spend more money! They have money. You just have to show them where to put it! Remember, YOU are the expert. If they could have stayed home and solved their problems, they would not have needed you in the first place. They came to you saying, "We have a problem. We NEED something that you have. We have money, and we want to trade it for something more valuable to us. Can you help us? Can you please take our money and solve our problems?"

Customers do not want to hear that you can only do SOME things for them. They want you to do EVERYTHING for them. You are the expert. You can do things they cannot do alone. Use your expertise to give them everything they want. Then, charge them for it!

I am constantly amazed at how DIFFICULT it can be to spend money. One Christmas, I was in a department store, trying to spend money. It was the 23rd of December, and I was in a mood to spend! There was an outfit on display that seemed perfect for my wife. Looking around, I spotted two sales clerks talking to each other at the cash register. They did their very best to ignore me. Even my waving and looking forlorn didn't work! They simply would not stop their conversation to give assistance.

So, I started shouting for help. "Help me, Help, Help, Help!", I shouted. That got their attention, (and the attention of quite a few other people as well.) They came rushing over and asked, "What is it? What is wrong?"

"I need help with that outfit. How much is it?"

It took them a second to catch on. They were quite upset. They were angry because I had shouted for help. Yet, that was why I was in the store in the first place.

Another example: My father owned a real estate agency with a fair number of sales associates, but no designated receptionist. When the phone would ring, he often had to answer it, because no one else would pick it up. His sales staff told him that the calls usually did not lead anywhere. He was astonished, (and he changed a few sales people)! So what if most of the calls did not lead to sales. If SOME of the calls brought in business, why wouldn't someone want them?

Take every opportunity to take your customer's money. Give them something of value, of course. But don't overlook the second purchase, the extra service, or the new product. If you need a lesson in this area, think of the fast food restaurants that have made MIL-LIONS by asking each customer, "Would you like fries with that?" Wouldn't you like to have an extra nickel from each order of fries McDonald's sells?

Customer Satisfaction And Profits

Remember, this chapter is about finding the *right* customer, who has the characteristics we discussed earlier. The right customer is also one who is compatible with the type and level of service and quality you offer. This will be reflected in your price, of course. If you have an inexpensive product or service, you will attract and ap-

15

peal to a certain type of customer. If you offer luxury and status, quite another type of person will make up the core of your business. You must create the strategies necessary to attract, and hold, qualified customers.

But no matter who your ideal customers are, there is one thing that is absolutely certain. You cannot make sustained, ever increasing profits, unless you are able to satisfy those customers. And, the more you satisfy them, the more they will pay you.

Don't ever fall into the trap of believing that making money is the opposite of satisfying customers. It is the exact same thing! If you want to make money, you MUST satisfy your customers!

And while we're on the subject of satisfying customers - which is easier - creating great customers from prospects, or creating great customers from good customers? I bet the second one is easier. You see - it is far easier to make a great customer of someone already familiar with the things you do best. If someone is currently your customer, you are already satisfying that person. Now, try to find some more things your customer would like.

The Price Dilemma

Are you afraid, or at least intimidated, by the prospect of asking people for money? This is a problem in our modern, corporate culture. As we create more and more layers of bureaucracy, we move further and further from the source of our profits - the customer. And, since most of us are trained to be "consumers" rather than "producers", we are unable to ask people for money. Let me give you a personal example.

A colleague and I were meeting with some prospective consulting clients. The man who owned the business had a lot of money, knew he had a problem, and wanted to hire someone else to fix it for him. This was a consultant's dream! Most of the time, our clients

16

either do not have enough money, or do not know they have a problem. Even if they have the first two, they simply don't want to hire someone to fix it for them. Instead, they try to do it themselves.

Back to our story. This guy really wanted to hire us. He wanted us to sign a contract and get started. However, my partner, who was senior to me at the time, did not ask for the business. Instead, he kept talking, telling the client how much better he would feel once he hired us to work on the project. It was almost too much for me to bear. I finally asked my partner to step outside with me. When we did, I said, "Stop talking and take this guy's money! He doesn't want to hear anything more about his problems. All he wants to hear is that we going to start solving them for him RIGHT NOW!"

We went back to the table and asked for a large deposit. The man was so relieved that it almost made me cry. However, when we got the check, which he wrote IMMEDIATELY, it made me want to dance and sing instead.

Your customers want to give you money. They simply want you to give them something of value in return. That is all they ask. Will they ever STOP asking you to give them something of value? No!

I hope you read this chapter carefully. It is really the most important part of this entire book. Once you understand that you are making money because you are doing something good for people, the whole game becomes a lot easier.

Trading Value For Value

Your customers have something. They have money. You want their money. But you knew that. And you have something your customers want. THEY WANT IT MORE THAN THE MONEY THEY HAVE!

Wow, read that again. They want what you have more than the money they have. That is it. Pack up your bags and go home, you do not need any more information. This is all there is to know. (Of course, the rest of the book contains specific suggestions for getting that money!)

You, as an expert, are adding value for your customers. You have trained, worked, planned, and organized all the resources necessary to make your customers happy. This has great value to them. And, they want to give you their money so you will transfer this value to them. They want what you have.

Unfortunately, they sometimes do not know what you have, or at least, they do not know ALL the things you have to offer them. So, you must tell them, or better yet, show them. We will talk about this some more in the next chapter. Suffice it to say that your job is to make sure that the customer knows EXACTLY what you can do for them.

Gathering Information

The key to discovering what your customers need, filling their needs, and charging them for it, is to first know as much as you can about your customers. Who are they? Where do they live? How much can they spend? What are their problems? This information is vital to offering products and services to meet their needs. But where do you find this information? How can you get it?

Here is a clue. You already have much of this information! It is in your business records. Simply begin to gather the extra data you need by looking at what you already have.

A casino hotel in Las Vegas had a gigantic Western-style clothing outlet attached to it. They had A LOT of customers, but didn't know much about them. We suggested a simple survey form for gathering some more information. The form only had four questions on it. They were:

1. Male or female (Don't worry, we didn't actually ASK this question. We used our observations.)

2. What state, or foreign country are you from?

3. If from out of town, what hotel are you staying in?

4. What time of day are you shopping? (Again, this was our observation.)

We put these books of questionnaires at the cash registers, spreading them out over weekends, weekdays and different times of day. In about two weeks, we had a LOT of information about the customers. We combined this with reports from the credit card companies, who told us what the average card holder was spending on retail clothing in our area. It was the start of a great database.

How about your business? What do you know about your customers? Are they returning to your business and remaining loyal? Do they use your products and services frequently or infrequently? What do they really want?

Do You Have A Friend?

Who are your best potential customers? They are probably very similar to your best customers right now. Go find some more of them! Study your current, best customers, find out where they are from and how they found out about your company. Then go find some more people just like them.

Rewarding Customers

I live by some very strict business rules. They involve honesty, caring, determination and persistence. Yet, the most important rule of all is one I call "Bill's Rule". Bill's rule is this: *People will not consistently do something for you unless you can show them what is in it for them.* Does that make sense?

Your customers want to know what is in it for them. Don't wait for them to discover it on their own. Tell them. Show them how you are rewarding them for their loyalty and their good taste! Give them something, and tell them you are giving it to them. This will increase their loyalty even more.

Everyone wants to feel special and appreciated. So, give your great customers something extra. It doesn't have to be expensive, just SOMETHING that shows you appreciate their business. Don't give them discounts. Give them an opportunity to satisfy more of their needs by purchasing more from you. Now there is a great philosophy.

Airlines have long used the frequent flyer programs to reward their customers. Do these programs save the flyers money? Maybe, but, that is not why the customers are using those programs. They want to fly MORE. And do they fly alone? Not usually. No, they take friends and family with them. In fact, they fly more than they would have flown if they did not have the program. This, in turn, means more business for the airlines.

Some people trade their frequent flyer points in for a first class upgrade. Others use them to buy companion tickets. Some, but not many, use them for free business travel. But those are the exceptions. And, of course, the use of the frequent flyer tickets is so restricted that it is almost IMPOSSIBLE to use them for business travel.

So what have the airlines done? They have created loyalty by giving a reward. The reward they give is not costly, because the person who earns the mileage, usually a business traveler, cannot use the tickets for traditional business travel. So, people take vacations with it, traveling on off-peak hours and days. But, don't ask one of these travelers to give up their frequent flyer miles. "This is one of the few benefits of BEING a business traveler" they will tell you - they LOVE those free miles. So do the airlines.

How can you reward your best customers? Remember that they don't want a discount. They want a reward! Why not reward them by giving them an opportunity to buy more?

Money Making Strategy #2
Finding The Best Customers For Your Restaurant

Carefully describe your best customer. What is it about that person that makes them so valuable to you? What does your restaurant do that gives this customer such great satisfaction? In other words, what value do you give them, and what value do they give you?

Now, how can you reward that person so they will remain loyal?

Don't even think about giving them a discount! Remember - your reward should give them more opportunities to spend money. Maybe you can create a special menu or seating area for them. Perhaps they should have priority on reservations. Be creative!

Chapter 3
The Only Two Ways To Make More Money In Your Business

Sponsored By

Energy-Efficient Solutions From TECO Energy

1. Cut Costs
2. Sell More

That's it! Did you think this would be more difficult? Remember, this is not rocket science. (Well, of course, if you ARE a rocket scientist...)

In this chapter, we will examine each of these two strategies, in a broad sense. Later, in the chapters that deal specifically with "the ten places where money is hidden", you'll find some ideas that are either cost cutting, or increase sales. In either case, you'll be operating on sound business principles.

How Money Is Made

If you are in business now, you already know how money is made. You sell things for more than you paid for them. When you buy raw materials, assemble them and create a product, then sell them for a fair price, you make money. In a service-oriented economy, this is even easier to do, because the cost of information and service is often very low. Yet, the selling price can be terrific. You see, it doesn't matter what it costs you to produce something. It only matters what VALUE it has to your customers. The greater the value, the more you can charge for it. The more you charge, the greater the perceived value!

Your customers are not interested in what it costs you to serve them. Remember, they really don't want the money they have. The money does them no good. They want to trade their money for things that are more valuable to them than the money they give you. As a business person, especially one who is committed to MAXIMIZING the profits from you endeavor, you are simply buying low and selling high. The only difference between you and other business people is that you are adding more value to your products and services. This let's you do two things. First, you can satisfy your customers better. Second, you can charge more. This helps to uncover the hidden money.

Who Has The Money?

You may wonder WHERE this "hidden money" is. Who has it? Why are they hiding it? The answers to the first question, "Where is it?", are given in chapter six of this book. We have researched the possibilities, and come up with some <u>great</u> ideas.

The answer to the second question, "Why are they hiding the

money?", is much easier. But before we answer that question, let's discuss the identity of these people who have your money.

Basically, there are two groups who have your money right now. They are your *suppliers* and your *customers*. Remember, the only two ways to uncover the hidden money is either to cut costs (look to your suppliers), or to sell more, (to your customers, of course!) Both of these groups are sitting on large amounts of your money. It is well hidden, but rather easy to uncover. In fact, both groups WANT you to uncover it. They are happy when you are making more money!

Your suppliers want you to stay in business. Why? Because they want to sell you even more! And, how can they sell you more? Well, only if you are selling more to your customers. And your customers want you to sell them more, because this means that more of their problems get solved. They can get rid of that pesky money that is done them no good at all. They can trade that money to you for the things they want - the things that solve their problems!

Cutting Costs By Adding Value

You have lots of suppliers. They may be phone companies, electric companies, equipment manufacturers, paper suppliers, etc. In fact, anyone who sells you anything for your business is a supplier. You are their customer. They are looking at you the same way you look at YOUR customers. They think YOU have hidden money for them!

Each of your suppliers charges you a price for the things they sell you. Just like your customers, you have money that is doing you no good. So, you want to trade it to your suppliers for the things you need, the things that have more value to you than the money does.

 This is the secret to uncovering money by reducing costs. You don't have to pay less for something. You simply must obtain more value for it. Use your suppliers to help you make more money with "strategy 2", selling more. Tap into their expertise so that you get more value, then SELL that valuable resource to your customers at a higher price.

25

Let me give you an example. A friend of mine is a sales manager for a food company that supplies all sorts of things to restaurants and hotels. My friend is also a certified chef and a graduate of the Hospitality School at Florida International University. What type of value does he offer to his customers? Not only does he sell them food and supplies, he consults with them on menu changes, storage techniques, merchandising, etc. His customers benefit from his expertise, and therefore can offer their customers more value, (and charge them for it as well!)

Look at a retail shop. Do you see displays and promotional items that are not created by the individual store? Certainly. Who helps the retailer create these items? The supplier, of course. So cutting costs does not necessarily mean paying less for the PRICE TAG. Cutting costs also means getting more value from your suppliers.

Here is a definition to remember: Price is everything you give up to get what you want. Memorize this! It applies to your relationships with both your suppliers and customers. It is a true key - an absolutely powerful tool - for finding the money that is hidden all around you.

This information is so powerful, that if you use it consistently, you will create a great SURGE in your ability to uncover hidden money. You will be a *money-making machine!*

Remember, if you want to use cost cutting as a strategy for identifying and uncovering hidden money, learn to form strategic alliances with your suppliers. Think of the psychology behind this move. After all, both you and your supplier are in the same business. You are both in the business of serving YOUR customers. Make it a team effort.

In the previous chapter, we discussed the process of finding the BEST customer. If you want to reduce costs, you have to be the BEST customer for your suppliers. What can you do for them to make them value your business? "But that isn't fair," you may be saying. "Why should I have to prove my worth to a supplier? They should be coming to me!" Well, it depends on what you want to accomplish. Did you want to uncover hidden money, or did you want to make people come to you and beg you for your business? If you just want the ego trip, fine. But, if you are really serious about maximizing your profit, get a partner!

YOU should go out and look for your suppliers. Don't wait for them to come to you. Arm yourself with facts. How much will you be buying? How frequently do you order? What is the value of your business? These are all important to know.

Now, go to and INTERVIEW the people who wish to sell you things. Ask them what they can do for you that will help you add more value for your customers. This is a far better strategy than simply negotiating for a lower price. You want the price to be fair, not low. Isn't that how you would define YOUR best customer? USE your suppliers, don't abuse them. Remember, price is everything you give up to get what you want. So, if you hammer your suppliers for a lower price, they will have to cut something out. You want them to be in business with you for a long time.

More Cost Cutting

Now that you know one of the great secrets of business, we can discuss how to literally CUT costs. There are several places to look immediately. The first is wherever you are actually WASTING money. Money is wasted when you buy something you do not need, when you make a mistake, or when you are the victim of theft. Let's look at each of these categories:

1. **Buying things you do not need** - We have all done it. Something looks good. It is so tempting. The salesperson tells you it is absolutely PERFECT. But, if you don't need it, it costs you too much - whatever the price. Examine your purchasing records, or simply look in the storeroom. There they are!

2. **Mistakes** - We all make them. Why? Because we are human, that's why. If your business were only operated by perfect people, you would have been thrown out long ago. When you make a pur-

chase, ask yourself, "What value does this add to my business?" Of course, some mistakes may result in over ordering or worse yet, under ordering. These mistakes cost money. Lower your costs by improving your planning.

3. **Theft** - People steal. Do all people steal? Probably not. But so many people DO steal that it is often a major cost. Be vigilant. Try to KEEP people honest by making it more difficult to steal. Will you stop it entirely? No. Can you slow it down? Absolutely.

The Danger Of Reducing Costs

Reducing costs in the right way is excellent. It makes your business more efficient. But, lowering costs the WRONG way can result in dissatisfied customers. Remember our definition of price - everything you give up to get what you want. Don't give up quality, delivery, guarantees, etc. Your customers will get less value. Remember, you are the expert. Your customers trust you to be THEIR BUYER.

Selling More

Okay, so now you know how to cut costs - by getting more help for selling your products and services to your customers. Now it is time to discuss the selling process. Just how do you sell more? Who do you sell it to?

 There are basically three ways to sell more. First, you can acquire new customers. Second, you can sell more to your existing customers. Third, you can help your existing customers find more uses for your product or service. Each of these strategies will result in the same outcome - uncovering hidden piles of money!

Remember, we said that there were two groups of people who had hidden money. They are your customers and your suppliers. So, how do you get that money from your customers? By giving them something they want.

1. **New Customers** - There are two types of new customers. One group is made of people just like the customers you already have. What would your business look like, and what would the profit be, if suddenly, you had more people buying your product or service? Would that make a difference in your bottom line? I guess it would!

The other type of new customer is one that is completely different than the customers you have now. This is only possible if you come up with some kind of new product or service. What can your company do to attract new customers? Can your creative team design some new services that provide value and benefits, and therefore attract new people?

2. **Selling more to existing customers** - Are you filling ALL the needs and wants of your current customers? Why not ask them? Many business people, even very good ones, sometimes lose sight of exactly WHICH problem they are solving for their customers. The famous case is the man who tries to sell his customer a quarter-inch drill bit, because the customer says he wants a quarter inch drill bit. But really, that is not what the customer wants. That customer wants a quarter inch HOLE, not a drill bit. Yet, we constantly make the mistake of mixing up features and benefits. You probably will not have much success trying to sell your current customers additional features. Learn to sell additional benefits. Benefits solve problems. Simply charge your customer for those benefits.

3. **New uses for existing customers** - This is an excellent way to uncover hidden money. IF you have satisfied customers, show them new ways to use your product or service. A real estate agent may sell rental properties to a couple who bought a home through him a few years before. Airlines and hotels can get business travelers to return for holidays. Retail clothing stores can keep track of the types of clothing their customers are buying, then notify the customers about specials on similar apparel. It is just a matter of caring enough to keep in contact - and making the next sale. Customer records can hold information about birthdays, anniversaries, milestones in life, etc.

Whatever your strategy for selling more, there is a customer out there just waiting for your attention. It requires imagination and good record keeping. The best time to set up a future sale is when the customer has just made a satisfactory purchase. Get in the habit of inviting customers to return, looking for products FOR them, and turning those good customers into GREAT customers.

Money Making Strategy #3
Supply-Side Economics!

This is a two step process. First, make a list of EVERY supplier for your business. This may be time consuming, but it is generally an eye-opener as well. When I was a consultant to a restaurant in Louisiana, we were looking at all the monthly bills to determine who our suppliers were. We found that we were paying a monthly charge to a cold-storage house in New Orleans. No one had any idea what was stored there. It turned out to be 1,100 POUNDS of frozen crab meat. None of the present employees knew when the stuff had been ordered, or by whom. We had it tested and, guess what? It was still good! Needless to say, we had several weeks of specials in the restaurant - all featuring crab meat. It was found money!

The second step is to start phoning each and every supplier. Ask them how they can help you lower your costs and serve your customers better. Some may not have any ideas at all. Consider changing suppliers! Others will have programs in place. They will be more than happy to add value to your order by helping you serve your customers better. Keep these suppliers and become their best kind of customer.

Chapter 4
Creating The Creative Team
Sponsored By

Crystals International Inc.

(800) 237-7620

Supplier of premium dry beverages and cocktail mixers
to the foodservice industry worldwide
congratulates

Outback Steakhouse, Inc.

1999 recipient of the

Florida Restaurant Association

"Lifetime Achievement Award"

A few years ago, my wife and I took the kids to Disney World in
Orlando. Actually, at the time, we LIVED in Orlando, but we decided
to "do it up right" and take the kids to one of the Disney hotels for a
weekend stay.

While in our room, we turned on the "Disney Channel". As you
might suspect, information about the parks was presented. What
really caught my attention was the announcement for an attraction
at EPCOT Center, called "Innovations."

In an excited voice, the TV announcer said, "There are things at
Innovations that are beyond your wildest imagination!" I turned to

my wife and asked her, "What do you think is in there?"

"How should I know," she replied. "He just told us it is beyond our wildest imagination!"

That is the problem with really spectacular things - they are beyond our wildest imaginations. So, we have no idea what we are looking for. How could we, if we can't even imagine it?!

What's New?

We are all limited by our personal experiences. Most of us are really not able to look ahead, to create something that does not exist now. Oh sure, we can MARGINALLY improve something. In our businesses, we can come up with some ideas that are slight MODIFICATIONS of things that already exist. But only a few people are able to create something different - a breakthrough.

One of my great heroes is Thomas Edison. Almost everyone knows that he invented the light bulb. But do you know the story behind the light bulb? It is fascinating.

Edison tried filament after filament, trying to find one that would give a good quality light, would last a long time, and would be economical and practical. In fact, he tried about *800* different filaments before stumbling upon tungsten fibers. Imagine that, 800 filaments. How many would you have tried before declaring that it just couldn't be done? I think I could have gotten to maybe 30. At that point, I would have told friends the experiment was over. And, I would have been very confident when I made my announcement. I would be SURE it couldn't be built.

Not Edison. He tried 800 DIFFERENT filaments. And, here is the big question. How many filaments WOULD he have tried before giving up? I believe the answer is ALL OF THEM. He would not have given up until absolutely every possibility was exhausted. Then, he probably would have tried some of them over again.

Beyond His Imagination

But think about it. Edison didn't even know what a light bulb looked like. He didn't even know if a light bulb COULD be invented.

He had to go beyond his wildest imagination. He had to work in conditions, and with materials and procedures, that had never been used before. Isn't that incredible?

And, think about this. He could only work during the daytime. He hadn't invented the light bulb yet! How did he do it? What drove him? How could he keep going, ignoring the skeptics, trusting only in his own ability to discern the impossible dream that he could some-day push back the darkness?

I don't know. It is beyond my wildest imagination!

Compared To The Light Bulb...

How does your business compare to pushing back the darkness? Is what you do easier than inventing something that didn't even exist except in the minds of the visionary? Probably. I know MY job is easier. I am not worried about spending a lifetime on something that will never work. I have seen other people do what I do. It isn't so hard.

 Your task is easy, especially when compared to Edison's. What you have to do is uncover the hidden money that you KNOW is there. And you know who has it. Your customers and your suppliers have it. They want you to find it. Now, isn't that simple?

The money probably became hidden because people begin to get complacent. The business is running pretty well. You have a fairly good income stream. The customers appear to be happy and loyal. So, you begin to lose sight of the fire that can drive a business. Yes, you are making money. But you are leaving a lot uncollected. Now is the time to set a creative team in motion that can unleash their imaginations on a relatively simple problem.

Creativity And Innovation

James Higgins, Ph.D. is a man of many talents. He wrote three books on creativity and innovation. They are *101 Creative Problem*

Solving Techniques, Innovate or Evaporate, and *Escape From the Maze.* Jim is also an outstanding consultant and speaker. His books, which have become standard reading in many organizations, take readers through a complete training course in innovation.

Jim really got my interest with the title of the first book, *101 Creative PROBLEM SOLVING Techniques.* You see, that is what creativity is for. It is to solve problems.

There are reasons why problems exist. They exist because no one has found a way to solve them. In order to change the situation, you must come up with some new thinking. The process of looking at a problem and coming up with a list of solutions is called creativity.

We all know some creative people. They tend to be excitable and flighty - right? No. Creative people come in all sorts of personalities. Just because someone is quiet doesn't mean they are not capable of having the spark of great imagination within. ANYONE can be creative. It is simply a matter of letting go a little bit - of separating ourselves from the past and not being bound by it.

Here is a true story. A woman was showing her daughter how to cook a roast. She demonstrated how to cut the ends off each side of the roast before putting it into the pan. "Why do you do that?" asked the daughter. "I don't know," replied the woman. "It is just the way my mother always did it. She showed me how to cook a roast."

They phoned the grandmother to ask her why she cut the ends off the roast. "Well," said the older lady, "years ago, I had a roasting pan that was always too small. So, I had to cut the ends off the roast. You aren't still doing that, are you?"

We are trapped by our pasts. We have habits and practices that are VERY difficult to change. Aren't you always hearing, (and maybe even thinking or SAYING), "That is the way it has always been done. People like it that way. If it ain't broke, don't fix it." Those sayings initially seem to make sense, but they are really the same as cutting off the ends of the roast - making no sense at all!

The first step in being creative is to realize that it doesn't HAVE to be done a certain way.

But, while there may be lots of creative solutions to any problem, there may only be a few PRACTICAL solutions. Creativity that leads to a practical solution is called *innovation*. An innovation produces a permanent (or at least semi-permanent) solution to a problem. An innovation is something that WORKS.

You must apply the creative process to come up with an innovative solution to your problems. If you want to uncover the hidden money in your business, you must develop innovations. These are changes in the way you DO business. They may be changes in marketing, production, processing or customer service. But they are definitely changes in the SYSTEM, THE WAY YOU DO WHAT YOU DO.

A Team Approach

So, if creativity isn't enough to try to solve problems, then simply having some creative people on your staff is not enough either. It takes a team of people to develop innovations. I once conducted a marketing seminar for the International Special Events Society (ISES). Now, these are creative people. I asked each person to describe the most significant challenge his or her company was facing at that time. One man had a very astounding reply.

"We have all these creative people working for us. What we REALLY need is someone who can think INSIDE THE BOX. We have lots of terrific ideas, but we can not seem to put them into practice because we are all running on to the next project."

Here was a company with creativity, but without the sustained effort to produce innovation. What did they need? Someone who could use the ideas to CHANGE the way they did business. This man was WORRIED that his company would fail because they could not innovate. It is important for ANY company.

Put together a TEAM of people who not only think of new ideas, but can evaluate those ideas, select the best ones and put them to work for the solution of the problem. That is innovation.

The Nature Of The Beast

Before you can put together the creative team - the group of people who are going to help you uncover the money hidden in your organization, you must first understand WHY they will do it. What drives your people? It is not going to be the same for each person! Now isn't that a complicating factor?

People respond to their needs. Each one of us is totally unique, and therefore have different needs. But each of us is seeking one thing. There is one word to describe what every individual wants. That word is *more*. Whatever it is they have, they want more of it. You have to discover, by asking them, what they want. Then, show them how to get more of it! Link that reward to the accomplishment of the innovation necessary to uncover the hidden money.

Primarily, if you want people to help you find some hidden money, then money is a good reward. By now I know what you are saying. "In all the classes I had in college, they taught us that money is not a motivator." That IS true, in a sense. It IS true that they teach that in college. It is not true that money will not motivate people. It will. When they did the experiments that tested the theory that money did not motivate, they were comparing a slight difference in pay. In other words, they looked at the difference in motivation between someone making $10 per hour as opposed to someone making $11 per hour. Of course, THAT amount of money is not a motivator. But we are talking about potentially VERY BIG sums in this book. I want you to take the lid off any incentive program you have. Let people make a FORTUNE if they can think of ways to solve problems, and make an even LARGER fortune for your company.

Does that make you nervous? Does it sound kind of crazy? Well it probably does. Why? Because most of us are stuck in this corporate culture, that says that all jobs pay a certain amount of money. Further, it is believed, if someone suddenly makes a whole lot of money, they will leave the company and go somewhere else.

 Now think about this for a moment. If someone is making a whole lot of money working in your organization, WHERE ARE THEY GOING TO GO? They can't go anywhere else. They won't make as much money. Don't tell me that money isn't a motivator - especially if it is a LOT of money. Money isn't EVERYTHING, but it is definitely WAY AHEAD of a plaque and a thank you letter. THAT is the kind of reward that drives great people to the competition!

A Case In Point

This is a true story about the University of Central Florida in Orlando. (And believe me, if a UNIVERSITY can do this, ANY type of business can do it.) UCF started an incentive program for their employees. If anyone came up with an idea that saved the university money, that person would receive a PERCENTAGE of the savings - WITHOUT LIMIT - FOR THE FIRST YEAR. Further, the employee's BOSS would get a piece of the money, and, the people who would actually have to DO the thing would also get money. What a great concept.

If your boss gets money from your ideas, isn't she/he likely to ENCOURAGE you to spend time on idea generation? And what about the people who would actually have to put the idea into practice, (that is, the people who would turn the creativity into innovation). Don't THEY deserve something as well? Of course!

The best example of the program at work was the case of the huge lecture hall where the lights were never turned off. They were all on - weekends, holidays - whatever! Someone noticed this, and made a formal suggestion. An investigation of the problem later revealed that the lights were always on because there was no way to turn them off. The light switches had been covered up when a new blackboard was installed. The solution? Cut a hole in the blackboard to expose the switches. The employee who suggested that one got a nice chunk of money. Would he have bothered with the suggestion if there were no reward? Well, he probably would have MADE the suggestion to look into it, but undoubtedly, no one would.

If you want to have additional plaques and other knickknacks as a reward, fine. But give the innovators and the creative types something MEANINGFUL for their work.

The Process

There are five steps in the process of creatively solving problems with innovations. They are simple, yet crucial. But remember, rewarding the people who come up with and implement the solutions is still the most important step! The five steps are:

1. **Idea Generation** - Become known as someone who welcomes ideas. Don't judge them. There is plenty of time for that later. Just get all the ideas out on the table.

2. **Branching** - In a brainstorming session, use the creative team to "branch off" ideas with new, even more imaginative thoughts. Again, there are no wrong answers here. Encourage the process, and discourage judgement. Nothing kills an idea session quicker than someone who immediately tells you why it can't be done.

3. **Choosing** - Okay, you have been waiting for this. Now it is time to critically examine each idea for its possible implementation. But don't do this until all the ideas are on the table. And don't close out some new ideas just because you have moved on in the process!

4. **Implementation** - Here is where you need the innovators. Reward the people who will actually have to put this raw idea into practice.

5. **Evaluate and reward** - Set clear goals for the program. State the rewards in advance. If the goals are met, IMMEDIATELY give out the rewards. This will spur your team on to new ideas and innovations.

Now you have the structure to start innovating and finding all that hidden money. Don't forget, the people who have that money right now are your suppliers and customers. The people who are going to help you uncover the money are the members of the creative team. Let them share in the wealth.

Money Making Strategy #4
Let's Get Creative

This is a two part strategy. First, you will give your creative team some exercises to get them warmed up. Second, you will plan some policies for rewarding the team when they do create an innovation.

The Exercise

Gather your team together and ask them to answer the question, "What is half of eight?" Tell them to write their answers on a piece of paper and to come up with as many variations as possible. At first, they will all write down "4". But, as they think about it, they may come up with IV, Quattro, or some other way of expressing the number. Some may say "0" (which is the top half of eight) or "3" (which is the right half of eight). Give them time and let them get their minds in shape to turn loose their creativity.

After they have a few minutes for this part of the exercise, ask them to "Write down all the uses you can think of for a broom". Give them a few minutes, then divide them into small groups and ask each group to do the same thing. After a few minutes, point out to them that people have different perspectives. Ask them if they all thought of the same things. It is a great lesson in how to use other people's thinking to initiate further creativity.

Now, it is your turn. Carefully develop a policy that rewards innovation in your company. Clearly state the goals, the rewards and the method of determining the viability of the suggestions. Then, go to it!

Chapter 5
Getting Started

Sponsored By

Have you ever heard of inertia? It is a noun, meaning an inability to start something. When your car is standing still, it takes more gas to just START the wheels turning than it does to KEEP the wheels turning once you have gotten started. This is the key to any success - just getting started. It is the difference between success and failure, defeat or triumph.

How many business ventures were never even brought to market simply because their founders could not get started? The truth is, we will never know - because no one ever heard of them! Have you ever had an idea that really got you excited? Did you talk it over

41

with your friends, tell them about its appeal to the masses and its certainty to bring you HUGE returns? I am sure you did. EVERYONE does. However, some people just get started, while others never do.

This is not to say that all ideas are worthy of rewards from the marketplace. Certainly not. There are some really bad ideas out there. But, I can say with absolute surety that the worst idea you ever had - the worst return on investment you ever received - was from inaction. It is paralyzing.

Goal Setting

The reason that most people do not take action, even when they have a sure-fire, winning idea, is that they have nothing that drives them. Most people do not have written goals. It is an undisputed fact.

 Tommy Newburry, author of "Success Is Not An Accident" estimates that only one percent of the population has written goals. Yet, this one percent of the people controls an INNORDINATE amount of the wealth. Why? Simple! Once they have developed MEANINGFUL goals, and created a plan for ATTAINING those goals, they are DRIVEN to achieve them.

If Mr. Newburry is right, and I believe he is, then goal setting is a powerful force for determining the outcome of both your business and personal life. And yet, this compelling force is neglected by virtually 99% of everyone in the business world. Moreover, I can say with absolute confidence, that the only thing that helped me to become successful was to set tangible objectives for my life.

What about you? Do you have WRITTEN, SPECIFIC and therefore, POWERFUL goals? Or, will you simply put this book down and remain uncommitted to accomplishing your full potential in business?

A Personal Dream

My wife, Jeanne, and I had very specific goals. We were living in Orlando, Florida, in a reasonable home, raising our two terrific daughters. We had the average suburban existence. Most people would have told us to be content with what we had. Yet, I was not. I knew there was more money hidden all around me, and I just had to find it. So, we set out on a journey of goal setting and income building. It has taken us some time, but, through innovation and commitment, we have accomplished the majority of our major goals. In fact, we are in the process of resetting them right now. I need MORE goals, because we have the things we set out to get. Our lifestyle is now almost EXACTLY as we designed it.

I don't write these words to brag. In fact, some of you may have a GRANDER lifestyle than we do. We are certainly not "Donald Trump" wealthy. We are not even as rich as Ivana or Marla! But we have SUBSTANTIALLY altered our lifestyle by setting goals, and then taking steps to accomplish our dreams. Let me tell you a little about our journey. It may help you on yours.

First, I should tell you, I am legally blind. I have an eye disease that has left me without sight in the center of my eyes, and with limited vision everywhere else. So, I cannot read print, nor can I drive. It makes things a little more difficult, but that is simply one more part of the challenge.

Jeanne and I decided to make a change in our lives in the early 1990's. Both of us had been raised living on the water, and we knew we just had to get back to that type of life. We wanted to live somewhere with a boat in the backyard, and access to the beach and ocean at our fingertips. I LOVE to fish, so the idea of walking out the back door and throwing a line into the water was extremely exciting. Finally, I wanted to be somewhere I could use the waterways for transportation and exercise. That was our dream.

Now, that may not sound too good to you. That's okay. It is OUR dream. You can go get your own! We spent a lot of time thinking about EXACTLY what we wanted. In fact, we described it in writing and put it on a poster over my dresser in the bedroom. We even wrote it BIG so I could see it.

Every night, our goals were the last thing I saw before going to bed. Every morning, they were the first things I saw when I woke up. THEY DROVE ME! THOSE GOALS WERE SO COMPELLING THAT I WAS GOING CRAZY TRYING TO ACCOMPLISH THEM. I would wake up in the middle of the night, thinking about the things we wanted. They would be on my mind constantly. IT HURT not to have what I wanted.

We wanted our dreams so much that we actually took action. We worked harder than I thought we could, doing the things no one else seemed willing to do. We were driven. But, because we had developed our goals as a team, we were driven together, not apart. We still took time for the family. Yet, we always gave time to our dreams as well.

What do you think happened? We now live on an island in Biscayne Bay, with our boat in the back and the beach a half-block away. Access to the ocean by boat is only minutes down the Intracoastal Waterway. My office at Florida International University is on the water, about two and a half miles from my back dock. I travel there by kayak! That's right - my coat and tie go into a waterproof hatch in the stern. There is a shower and locker room in the first floor of my building. In fact, my unique way of commuting has been featured in the Miami Herald, and on local television.

How did we reach those goals? Well, the first step was to SET them! Then, we were able to identify exactly how much money it would take to achieve them. The rest was simple, although by no means easy. We looked for money in hidden places and then dug it out. But, it was the commitment to our goals that kept us going.

Time To Set Your Goals

Now, it is time to set YOUR goals. WHAT do you want? WHEN do you want it? Both of these questions are more important than *how* you will get it. You can always find ways to get money, or whatever else you want. The hard part is to build up the motivation necessary to keep you on track. That is where most people fail, before they even get started.

Perhaps you are completely content where you are now. Your business is producing all of the money you need. Your lifestyle is EXACTLY where you want it to be. In that case, put this book down and go fishing. There is no information for you here. On the other hand, maybe you are not looking for anything for yourself, but would like to help someone else achieve his/her goals. You can do that. All you have to do is find someone who wants the results strongly enough to do the work. Finally, maybe YOU want something more. In that case, write it down. Then, go and get it.

Start with small goals. But, write them down. Then, move to more creative goals. But, write them down. Finally, select some high-impact, far reaching goals. But, of course, write them down. There is no such thing as a compelling or attainable goal unless it is written down.

The Trouble In Setting Goals

Most people have difficulty in selecting large goals. The problem is, hardly anyone ever ASKS us what we want. Most people spend time TELLING us what they want us to do. How about where you work? Are you an inspiring person who will listen to other people's dreams? Have you ever asked someone what they want? Most of us do not. We are afraid of the answers! We are afraid that we can never meet the expectations of other people. There is no need to fear that anymore.

If you commit yourself and your business to a meaningful exploration of the true needs of your customers, you will find hidden money. It is inevitable. And, if you unleash the power of a dream in other people, and show them how they can share in the rewards, THEY will uncover the money for you. Ask them what they want, and then show them how to get it.

Let them have some of the money they uncover. Give them lots and lots of meaningful recognition. Don't recognize them for what they do for the company, recognize them for what they are doing for themselves! Talk about their accomplishments in terms of PERSONAL achievement. That will motivate them more.

It Starts With A Goal - And Ends With A Reward

In general, follow the steps listed below to implement the things you have learned from this book. They will lead you to the hidden wealth that is all around you. It may come from the most unexpected sources, or it may be from a traditional source in your business. In any case, BE READY FOR IT!

1. **Establish a REASON for uncovering the money** (Set specific goals)
2. **Form a creative team** (Ask them what THEY want)
3. **Talk about the rewards** (Make sure the rewards give people what they want)
4. **Gather customer information** (Do they get everything they need from your company?)
5. **Brainstorm for some ideas** (Remember to innovate, not just create)
6. **Choose a program** (But not until ALL the ideas are on the table)
7. **Make great customers out of good ones** (Increase revenue)
8. **Become a great customer to your suppliers** (Ask them for help)
9. **Evaluate your progress towards the goals** (It can't be done unless the goals are written)
10. **Reward, reward, reward** (And ask them if they want more!)

Are you ready to get started? Are you surprised to find out that you will be starting with a goal-setting session? Well, now you know. Everything worthwhile starts with a dream. So get started. Once you have your goals, use the ideas found in the book to start uncovering the hidden money. It is waiting for you.

Money Making Exercise #5
This Is What We Want!

This is a two-part exercise. First, write down your goals. Be specific. Don't spare the details. The more you write, the more REAL those goals will become. If you have a spouse or partner, work with them. Ask yourself: WHAT exactly do I want, and WHEN do I want it. Don't be shy. This is YOUR dream. Make it personal.

Now, ask at least two other people what THEY want. Help them develop their goals. They are probably shy as well. After all, it is unlikely that anyone has ever ASKED them before. Listen to them. Ask more questions. Become known as the type of person who is INTERESTED in helping others get what they want.

Now keep on practicing until you are a master GOALIE!

Chapter 6
10 Places Where Money Is Hidden
Sponsored By

HOPCO
FOODSERVICE
MARKETING
FOOD BROKERS SERVING
THE STATE OF FLORIDA
(813) 874-2500

You have set your goals. The creative team is in place, and they know what their rewards will be. Now get ready to create some new wealth!

None of the techniques you are about to read will require significant changes in your menu, your theme, or your staffing levels. They are all simple, yet powerful, FAST ACTING techniques for increasing both customer satisfaction and your profits.

Could you ask for more?

#1 Sell The Big Contributors

Sponsored By

FIU FLORIDA
INTERNATIONAL
UNIVERSITY
School of Hospitality Management

Success comes in degrees - -
Achieve your dream with a degree from FIU

Bachelor's Degree in Hospitality Management
Master's Degree in Hotel & Foodservice Management
Special Certificate Programs in Hotel/Lodging,
Restaurant/Foodservice or Travel/Tourism

3000 N.W. 151 Street, North Miami, FL 33181
Tel: (305) 919-4500 Fax:(305) 919-4555
Website: www.fiu.edu/~hospman
E-mail: hospman@fiu.edu

Are you concerned about the average check? How about the food cost percentage? Did you know that neither of these items is the most effective measure of where money is hidden on your menu? It's true. Of course, the average check is important. And the food cost percent is a fair measure of your efficiency, but neither one of these items REALLY contributes to your bottom line.

No, what you are looking for is contribution margin. Contribution margin is the difference between selling price and variable costs. You know what the selling price is for each item. It is on the menu. And, the variable costs are easy to calculate. They are the food costs, and to some degree, some labor costs, that make each item saleable. You are looking for the items with the largest contribution margins. That is what you want to sell.

51

Let's take a simple example. Suppose your restaurant only has three menu items. They are listed below, with their selling prices and variable costs.

Item	Price	Cost	Contribution Margin
Steak	$12	$5	$7
Chicken	$10	$2	$8
Pasta	$ 9	$2	$7

In the simple analysis above, we see that the item with the highest contribution margin is actually the chicken. But, which item would your WAITER rather sell? The one that gives the highest check average, of course. This will give him/her a better tip. So, it is possible that the most advantageous item for the house is not the one the waiter will push.

Contribution margin falls right to the bottom line. It is one of the MOST important places where money is hidden in a restaurant. It is important for two reasons. First, there is a lot of money hidden in those items! Second, and perhaps more importantly, understanding contribution margin analysis is fundamental to managing a restaurant profitably.

How can you successfully use contribution margin information to uncover hidden money? The first step is to actually DETERMINE what the information is, by conducting a sales mix analysis.

Create a spreadsheet, either by hand or on a computer. (Actually, the table above is a spreadsheet.) On the spreadsheet, list all the items you serve, including desserts and appetizers. To the right of each item, list its selling price, cost, and contribution margin per item. Also list the number sold each week, (get this information from the guest checks), and the total contribution margin per item, (multiply the contribution margin for that item by the number sold). If we used the chart above, it may look something like this:

Item	Price	Cost	Contribution Margin	# Sold	Total Contribution
Steak	$12	$5	$7	40	$ 280
Chicken	$10	$2	$8	90	$ 720
Pasta	$ 9	$2	$7	100	$ 700
Total				230	$1,700

In this simple sales mix analysis, the restaurant sold 230 dinners for a total of $1,700 in contribution margin. That is an average contribution margin of $7.39 per person.

Yes, I understand that your sales mix analysis will be vastly more complicated. But, can you see the money hidden here? Once you establish your average contribution margin, you can IMMEDIATELY set about raising it. There are two strategies:

1. Sell each person more "extras". This will raise the average contribution, and if you have good food, make your customers happier.

2. Change the sales mix. Train your waiters to SELL THE BIG CONTRIBUTORS!

#2 Let Me Introduce You To 200 Of My Closest Friends

Sponsored By

Stewart Smith Southeast

and

Third Party Administration

Congratulates
Outback Steakhouse, Inc.
on their induction into the
Florida Restaurant Hall of Fame

Who are your very best customers? What do they order? How often do they visit your restaurant? Answering these questions is the basis for "VIP Marketing". What is it? Quite simply, VIP marketing is relationship building. It means you know the names, and the purchasing habits, of the most important people to your restaurant. It requires some organizational skills, some imagination, and a total dedication to the people who will become your ambassadors.

The first step is the hardest. How will you track your customers? What criteria will you use? Who will do the work?

Let me suggest the following: enlist the help of your creative team. Let them develop the criteria used to put people into the top group. Frequency of visit is a good place to start, but your restaurant may have some other factors, such as average check or size of party. Whatever you use, start to measure your guests against the standard. Obviously, you won't treat the average patrons in a poor manner, but you will LAVISH attention on your top performers!

Once you have selected your top customers, start putting together a data base about them. Don't let that word "data base" scare you. It doesn't have to be a computerized system. You can use file cards, loose leaf binders, or the back of a slow moving busboy to keep the records. You want certain information, such as birthdays, family members, personal preferences, etc., on each of the files. When one of these elite guests DOES show up, refer to the file and get to work.

At the Breakers Hotel in Palm Beach, they use a system like this for ALL their repeat customers. For example, when a customer calls room service, his or her name is automatically pulled up on a computer screen. If the name has an asterisk next to it, it means that the customer has made a special request in the past. It may be something simple like "hot sauce with the eggs". Whatever the special need, the customer is accommodated without asking. However, the customer is TOLD "I understand you like hot sauce with those eggs. We will put some on the tray for you." (What's the sense in doing something good if you don't tell the customer you are doing it?!)

The *Cornell Hotel and Restaurant Administration Quarterly* recently reported a story about a man who saved his business through VIP marketing. Manfred Esser completely turned around the fortunes of Cuvaison Wineries by practicing what he called "Guilt Marketing". Esser identified the top 200 customers, and made them such strong allies that they felt guilty if they bought any other wine! For example, he sent them live grape vines to plant at their homes. This made them part of the Cuvaison Grape Growers Association.

The famous Oriental Hotel in Bangkok sends its top 200 customers a bottle of Dom Perignon on their birthdays, NO MATTER WHERE THEY ARE IN THE WORLD ON THAT DAY! How would your customers feel about that kind of treatment?

Now, maybe you can't afford to send fancy champagne, (or maybe your customers don't drink champagne), but there are many innovative things you CAN do to honor these great contributors to your bottom line, and to keep them coming back!

1. Let them order OFF the menu. Keep a little something in reserve for these people. Does your chef have a specialty that isn't usually on the menu? When you get in some special ingredients, perhaps a phone call to your top customer list will bring them back.

2. Celebrate with them. Keep them on a card list. Send them congratulations. Read the local paper and keep an eye on their accomplishments.

3. Give them seating priority. Don't make them stand in line with the average customers.

You want these people to feel like they are a part of your restaurant's family. If they go somewhere else, they should feel guilty about it. After all, they know how important they are to you!

#3 Quick, I Need More Tables In Here!
Sponsored By

James M. Higgins & Associates, Inc.
800-266-8283

Offering comprehensive initiatives for improving:
Strategic growth through product/service innovation,
and efficiency management through process innovation.

"Changing the Rules of the Game"

Restaurants, like most businesses, have a capacity problem. When it is busy, you need more seats. But building a dining room large enough to accommodate your biggest demand is not practical. Think of the costs to construct it, let alone maintain it during slow times. Instead, here are a few ways to suddenly, and in some cases, dramatically, increase your seating capacity.

1. **Community table** - Back in the 1970's, I was visiting a southern town for a business meeting. I was alone, and it was lunchtime. I didn't relish the idea of going into a nice restaurant by myself, having to sit at a table with no one to talk to. However, I'd heard of a great place, and I was hungry, so I went. The hostess greeted me, and noticing I was alone, said, "Would you like to sit at the Gentlemen's Table?"

59

The Gentlemen's Table was actually a series of 6-foot tables, placed end to end, with chairs all around. It was for single diners, (men or women), or even small groups, who wanted to sit at a community table and meet other local business people. Each of us received an individual check. What a great idea! It automatically increased capacity, delighted the customers and gave the place a great reputation. (One word of caution, however. Remember, this story took place in the 1970's. Don't call it a "Gentlemen's Table" today. It would be politically incorrect!) Whatever you call it, use the idea to create capacity during high demand.

2. Limit the menu - Want to get people off those tables, and get some new diners down? Consider a limited menu during peak times, or even better, on holidays or special occasions. It increases the capacity of your kitchen, moves customers through by speeding up their ordering process, and gives you the ability to make more money.

A limited menu doesn't necessarily mean limited quality or excitement. Try an all inclusive menu that gives the customers a real show, lots of great food, but still only lets them choose one item from column A, etc. Use your imagination. This technique can be a real reputation builder!

3. The Grand Buffet - Whether it is a salad bar, or a beautiful grand buffet, the concept can increase your capacity. First, you need fewer servers. Second, people are more likely to sit in groups. Third, you can seat people all over the restaurant, and they still have a great dining experience. These buffets can be real popular!

The down side is that guests may stay longer. So, even though you increase your capacity, you may lose the ability to move them out quickly. However, most restaurants have found that the advantages in seating, satisfaction and revenue are greater than the increased dining time.

4. Take that outside! - Don't overlook the popularity of outdoor dining. A nice tent can accommodate even fine dining. I was recently the pre-dinner speaker to a group of meeting planners who met at Donald Trump's *Mar A Lago* in Palm Beach. The dinner was held on the grounds, in a beautiful, tented dining room. It was elegant - and memorable!

5. **Use the bar** - Don't overlook the non-dining spaces in your establishment. A limited menu in the bar, or a banquet room, will give patrons a nice choice, and give you some uncovered profits!

6. **Let's have our coffee in the drawing room** - Want to build a reputation while making more money? Create a special dessert and coffee area. Invite guests to move from their tables after dinner. Give them complimentary coffee, and sell them desserts and drinks. Why not theme the room with jazz music and an after-hours ambience?

Your chance to suddenly "build more seats" is a great key to finding hidden money. You can sustain that increase in revenue by enhancing your reputation for a different dining experience.

#4 Increasing Food Costs

Sponsored By

SCHWAN'S FOOD SERVICE

One of the most misleading ratios used in restaurants today is the food cost percentage. Yet, it is often used as a measure of the operation's efficiency and productivity. At the end of the year, however, you don't take your luxury vacation based on the food cost percentage. You take it based on the amount of satisfaction you gave your guests! That may have absolutely NOTHING to do with the food cost. In fact, controlling your food cost - to the exclusion of other considerations - can actually cost you money. There are some great profits hidden in the food cost percentage. Let's go get them!

I am speaking from personal experience! I set a food cost percentage of 35% for my restaurant in New Jersey. Each menu item was priced to reflect that percentage. Unfortunately, life just doesn't work like that. At breakfast, for example, my ham cost much more than my bacon did. In order to keep my food cost percentages in line, I had to cut the ham so thin you could read a newspaper through it! I created MASSIVE customer dissatisfaction.

Okay, so you are smarter than I am. You use an average food cost percentage that takes into account all the various menu items. Well, that makes more sense, but it is still the wrong concept. Even worse, it may cause you to overlook some hidden money. Here is why.

Suppose you have a menu where steak sells for $15, and costs you $5 to make. This is a 33% food cost. You also have a chicken dish that sells for $10 and costs $3 to make. This is only a 30% food cost. But, which one would you rather sell? The steak, which has a higher cost percentage, also has a higher contribution margin! Every time you sell a steak, you make $10. Every time you sell a chicken, you only make $7. Which would you rather make?

The average person only has one entrée, so you want to maximize the potential each time they dine with you. You do not want to MINIMIZE the potential by selling the items that meet your food cost percentage.

Consider this philosophy. You want to control costs, of course. But you want to control them in such a way that they make your guests happy! The question you should ask yourself is, "How much will it cost me to meet my guests' expectations?" You are still controlling costs, but this subtle difference in philosophy can make a HUGE difference in the bottom line.

Now, consider the other end of the food cost percentage equation - the price. Could you change the prices, either directly or indirectly, and sell more of the big contributors? You know how to directly affect the price. You can lower the cost of the steak, or raise the price of the chicken. Either way, the customer may be more tempted to buy the steak. They could think, "Well, it is only a dollar more for the steak. That is what I really want." If you accomplish this by raising the price of the chicken, you win either way!

Indirectly, you can change the price by offering a special that combines several menu items, such as appetizer, entrée, and dessert. Present them to your customers at a special package price.

This will increase the food cost percentage, but it may also increase the average contribution margin, because the customer actually spends more than he might have if everything was a la carte. It also has the potential to increase guest satisfaction by creating a meal-time "experience" for your guest.

Spend as much as you need to spend in order to create satisfied customers, great menus and big profits. Go ahead, that money is waiting for you. Uncover it!

#5 Sorry, That Seat Is Taken

Sponsored By

It is time to stop giving away one of your most precious resources - a seat in your restaurant - to any party that walks in. Your seating arrangement cannot be changed very easily. Of course, you can push a deuce and a four-top together to make a six-top, but a big booth for six just can't be changed. There is a lot of money hidden in the way you accept reservations, assign seats, and treat walk-ins.

Of course, this discussion applies primarily to the times when your restaurant is full, or nearly so. For some real detailed information on this subject, please refer to an article I wrote for the Cornell Hotel And Restaurant Administration Quarterly, titled *Making More Money In Your Restaurant*. The article is in the June 1999 issue. For right now, though, let's keep it simple.

Let's look at two examples of using seat assignment to uncover some hidden money. It's Friday night in a mythical restaurant, Quain's, and the joint is jumping! A party of six wants a reservation that will require you to put a two-top and a four-top together. You must decide whether to accommodate them, or hold those two tables open in hopes that a four and a deuce will want them. Luckily, you have kept a record of all the reservation requests and walk-in business that you normally get on a Friday. (I suggest you START keeping this information if you do not have it.) Also, you have kept records on the average dining time and average check for different party sizes. Using this information, you make the following decision:

You turn down the reservation, (or try to steer them into a "down time"), because your records show that a party of six takes about one hour and a half to eat, while a deuce and a four only take about an hour each. Also, the average check (or contribution margin if you use it) is about 10% less per person for the larger party. You can make more money if you turn the smaller tables.

In the second situation, you have an open booth for up to six people. It is the middle of the Friday dinner rush. You do not take reservations, and a party of four is next in line for a table. You know, from your records, that you are very likely to get a party of six as a walk-in. Your decision is:

Save the booth for a larger party and let the party of four wait. You decide not to give the booth away when you are pretty certain that a larger group will walk in at any minute. (Obviously, you have to handle this situation discreetly. However, you want to uncover that money don't you?!)

You will notice that in both of these cases, you are taking a chance. You may lose a "sure thing" in the hopes of maximizing your profit. But, with some attention to record keeping, you can build up a base of information that will let you make better and better decisions.

Even if you do not change your seating policy, the information you gather about dining time, average check and party size will lead you to other sources of hidden income.

The objective is to maximize the use of your resources. So, if you have a 100-seat restaurant, you want to have 100, high-profit, quick-turning customers in those chairs during your busiest times. This will give you the greatest return on your investment.

For example, if your busiest time is between 7 and 8 p.m., you certainly want your restaurant to be filled to capacity at those times. The trick is trying to get enough fast turning tables filled as close to 7 as possible. This may enable you to take another seating BEFORE the crowd begins to disperse. Get that creative team to work on this right away!

#6 Hey, That's Our Specialty
Sponsored By

Bill Quain, Ph.D.
Profit Generation through Innovation

Looking for a kick-start in your search for hidden money? Why not work with the revenue professional who wrote the book on the subject?

Contact Bill Quain for a customized program of money generating ideas.

(305) 944-7673
bill@quain.com

Every restaurant, no matter how small or large, moderately or take-a-second-mortgage-on-the-house-so-we-can-dine-there priced, MUST have a specialty. Each property needs something that sets it apart from the competition, and makes it memorable.

Why?

Because, the guest is buying more than just the food. Your patrons are looking for an experience. They want to know what you are, and what it is you do best. Here are some specialties that restaurants all over the country are using to uncover hidden profits, and to increase guest satisfaction.

1. **Quick service** - Do you have a clientele that requires fast service? Perhaps it is a morning rush hour, a lunchtime crowd, or a dinner segment that needs to finish a meal before the theater. Quick

service does <u>not</u> have to mean a burger and fries. (Although, MIL-LIONS of dollars have been made serving burgers to fast-food customers. By the way, don't forget to ask, "Would you like fries with that?") A specialty in quick service is required whenever there is a time constraint. Your restaurant, if it becomes known for dependability and consistency, can attract LOTS of customers who simply need to be finished dining by a certain time. *Don't miss your curtain call!*

2. **Themes** - A theme can be extravagant, or relatively subdued. Victoria Station Restaurants really got the theme syndrome going in the sixties. Since then, a wide variety of themes have proliferated. But, don't stop with the décor when you plan your theme. Match up specialty food and beverage items and SELL them. Give the guest the full experience, and let them pay you for it.

3. **Portion size** - How about making a name for yourself by WOWING people with the food you give them. As the food and beverage director at a ski area near Lake Tahoe, I started "Colonel Quain's Poultry Palace". We gave our patrons paper plates, and sent them down a line of charcoal grills to pick up their food. The last thing that went on the plate was a half chicken. It was a huge portion and, very often, the plate would dip as the tasty fowl was laid on. We got the same reaction each time - "WOW"!

4. **Food items** - What is the one thing you do better than anyone else's restaurant? I hope there is something! You should choose one or two items and stake your reputation on them. Put everything you can into the quality of these dishes, starting with the selection of the very best raw ingredients, and ending with a flourish as the item is served. Perhaps it is a prime rib that is served tableside, or a salad bar that goes on forever. Why not consider a Sunday brunch, or a hard to prepare menu item that is simply outstanding. Give them something they cannot get at home.

5. **The Big Secret** - When all else fails, use a secret sauce. Make it something special. This works for all kinds of restaurants. And, in today's market, customers want a variety of tastes. A Mexican restaurant in Orlando has a selection of twenty hot sauces available

from a "sauce bar". My favorite is a real stomach burner called "Slap My Ass And Call Me Sally". No kidding!

6. **Off the menu** - Why not create a series of specials that can be offered to guests, even though they are not on the menu. Wouldn't you like to take friends to a place where the waiter says "Well, this isn't on the menu, but I know the chef just got in some great duck. I am sure I could get him to make a special dish for you tonight." Everyone wants to feel special.

7. **Service** - Is there something truly special about your service? Do your customers recognize you for the difference you create every time they sit down? Consider table-side preparation, nicknames, costumes, shows - something that makes your staff special. It may simply be that they know how each dish is prepared. If that is the case, tell the guest. Let the staff show their talents. No matter what type of restaurant you have, there should be SOMETHING about your service that is unique and memorable - and, most importantly, that adds to the satisfaction of the guest.

Specialize in something. Make it appropriate for your level of pricing and service. Tie it into the menu and design your specialty to sell more product, not just to create a memory. Remember, your guests want to FIND a place that does something special. They want to be in on a secret. There is no better advertising than having a solid group of patrons who will tell their friends, "I have GOT to take you to this place I found. It's great!"

The key to specializing is to pick a set of specialties that increase guest satisfaction by enhancing the total experience, and by giving the guests the opportunity to spend more money, more often.

#7 Ask, And You Shall RECEIVE
Sponsored By

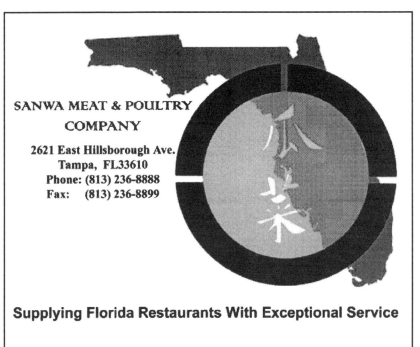

SANWA MEAT & POULTRY
COMPANY

2621 East Hillsborough Ave.
Tampa, FL33610
Phone: (813) 236-8888
Fax: (813) 236-8899

Supplying Florida Restaurants With Exceptional Service

One of the most important aspects of food service is to purchase the right products. Your guests deserve fresh, wholesome and high-quality ingredients. Yet, too often, the manner in which restaurateurs RECEIVE the food is haphazard. Sure, they spend a lot of time developing specifications, working with suppliers and demanding quality. Yet, when the food actually arrives, it may be signed for, put away, and to some degree, forgotten. It is time to work with suppliers as partners, rather than simply delivery men.

Here is an example of what happens in some restaurants. (I know, because it happened in MY restaurants!)

It is 11:30 a.m. The kitchen is in its usually CRAZY state, getting ready for the lunch crowd. And here it comes - not the lunch crowd, but the delivery truck. Suddenly, there are boxes and cases at the back door and a driver with a clipboard. What do you do?

Too often, I yelled to a dishwasher, "Joe, check in that order. I am too busy trying to get a busboy out of the storage closet. He's sleeping on the tablecloths again."

Joe goes over to the deliveryman, who thrust the clipboard at him. "It's all here," says the driver. "See? There are four cases over there, two on the table and I put four in the storage room for you. Sign here."

Well, maybe this is a slight exaggeration, but there are many challenges in the process of INSPECTING the food you have purchased. Here are a few hints that can both SAVE you money and MAKE you money:

1. Work with a reputable supplier. Become that supplier's best customer and expect them to treat you like one!
2. Get help from your sales person. You need a knowledgeable partner. Ask him or her to periodically accompany the delivery.
3. Clearly state the TIMES when you will accept deliveries. Be firm.
4. Assign a responsible, TRAINED person to receive your food stocks.
5. SEPARATE ordering and receiving functions. Don't let the same person order the food, then receive it. (Unless you do both yourself. But, you still need to train a back up.)
6. Inspect all foods. Weigh, count, and smell!
7. If something does not meet your CLEAR, WRITTEN standards, SEND IT BACK!
8. If there is a "short", get a credit slip. Ask the driver to sign it.
9. If there is a problem with your order, especially one that will affect your ability to serve your guests, CALL THE SALESPERSON IMMEDIATELY.
10. Keep accurate records. Check the price you are billed against the quantity you received, the price you were quoted, and the delivery receipt.

Your reputation as a careful and concerned buyer will help you in two ways. First, you will save money by becoming a better customer. Your supplier will respect your concern for quality products. By developing a "partner" relationship, you and your supplier can depend on each other for consistency and fairness. This will cut your costs.

Second, you will be confident that you will have the right amount of food, and the correct quality of that product, to meet the needs of your guests. They will develop confidence in your consistency, leading to increased sales.

#8 Make Them <u>Have</u> To Say "No"

Sponsored By

Here is a real change from our usual practice! We are always telling restaurateurs to give the guests a reason to say "yes" - "yes" to big contributors, extra services, celebration amenities, etc. In this case, we are going to require them to say "no" to extra items.

I got this idea while taking a cruise last year. Each night, when we arrived at our table, there were two bottles of wine sitting there. One was a nice, chilled white. The other was a carefully selected red. Both of them fit into the theme of the dinner for the evening, and were appropriate for various menu items. The wines weren't FREE of course. If the guest wanted them, they had to pay. (You understand that this is a GOOD thing from your perspective as a restaurateur!)

The key, is that everyone had to make a decision about those bottles of wine. Instead of saying "yes" to a waiter's suggestion of the wine from a wine list, each table of guests had to say "NO" in order to get rid of the bottles. Many tables did refuse them - on the first night. On the second night, fewer people said "no". As we settled into the routine of the ship, it became easier and easier to just accept the suggested wine and enjoy it.

This same principle can be applied to so many items. Darrell Wilde, Assistant Director of Food and Beverage at the *Breakers Hotel* in Palm Beach, tells of their incredible success with desserts. On an average night in their steak restaurant, they would sell desserts to about 10% of the diners. Darrell did not consider this to be an acceptable percentage.

The management decided it would be better to have the guest refuse a dessert then to actually request one. So, they constructed a very visible dessert cart, with a wonderful display of pastries, pies and cakes. The cart was wheeled around the dining room. It was so beautiful, that it really became part of the excitement of dining in this restaurant. And to make it even more appealing, the restaurant's managers made it even harder for the guests to say "no" by using a simple, yet elegant approach.

There were so many wonderful choices on the cart that some guests would say "no", simply because they couldn't decide. So, the Breaker's staff created a dessert combination. For the same price as a full piece of one dessert, the diners could get a small slice of EACH dessert. Now, who could say "no" to that?

Under the dessert cart program, dessert sales increased from 10% to 40% of all diners in the steak house. Imagine what an increase in dessert sales like that can mean to the bottom line! Desserts are generally high contribution margin items. Certainly, the average contribution margin per person SHOT UP in the restaurant.

What can you do in YOUR restaurant to improve the bottom line? Are there places where money is hidden because you are forcing the guests to say "yes" rather than making it impossible, OR UNNECESSARY, to say "no"? Think of the items that could increase the per person contribution margin, and at the same time, increase guest satisfaction. Remember that increased sales can only be sustained if guests are satisfied with the total product at your property. Which guest is more satisfied with the TOTAL experience? Is it the person who has an entrée only, perhaps with a glass of water, or is it the diner who enjoys a bottle of wine, appetizer, dessert, and the entrée? If your guests are not taking full advantage of your menu, then you either have the wrong menu, the wrong approach, or the wrong guests. (See the chapter on finding the right guests for more information.)

Put your creative team to work on this one. The money is there, just go dig it out. You will increase customer satisfaction AND make a positive impact on the bottom line. What could be better?

And, if you are still at a loss for ideas for your restaurant in this area, go take a cruise. Or, look up Darrell Wilde at The Breakers. Either way, you are going to come out a winner!

#9 See You Later (Or Earlier)
Sponsored By

The Institute for Hospitality and Tourism Education and Research
At
Florida International University's
School of Hospitality Management

Dedicated to providing educational and research opportunities to members of the international, national, state, regional, and local Hospitality, Tourism, and Travel Industry communities, students and graduates of the School.

For more information about the Institute contact:

Professor Joan Remington—Director
Institute for Hospitality and Tourism Education and Research
FIU—School of Hospitality Management
3000 N.E. 151st Street—HM 216
North Miami, Florida 33181-3000
Phone: 305-919-4514 Fax: 305-919-4555
e-mail: ihter@fiu.edu
Or access the Institute's web site at: www.fiu.edu/~ihter

You are undoubtedly already using some parts of this technique. But many restaurants miss a golden opportunity here as well. I am talking about spreading demand over the entire time your property is open. This usually takes the form of an "early bird" special. Yet, there are some other ways to utilize your existing facility and resources that are not so common.

I live in south Florida, so early birds are well known here. I think the average age of the patrons is about 709. During the winter season especially, these oldsters start lining up outside some of the great restaurants down here, looking for the terrific deals, and getting home in time to watch the early news on television.

Of course, almost all restaurants can use this technique, even if you are not catering to the geriatric set. The object is to spread

83

demand out so that the capital investment in seating and the building, along with the labor you need to have in order to meet the later dinner rush, will all be utilized to their fullest. It makes sense.

But, what about the other end of the evening? There are great opportunities to offer a "late owl" special, that will keep your staff busy while the restaurant gets ready to close. I suggest a limited menu - or maybe even a completely DIFFERENT menu for this crowd. It can be difficult to serve a full menu right up until closing. So why not create an easy-to-serve, yet unique and highly profitable menu for the late owls?

Is there a theater near your restaurant? Are people getting off work from a late shift? Are there Europeans or other tourists who might be in the habit of eating later? Each of these segments can make a great clientele. And, the late owl menu could be a unique positioning tool for you as you create your "special" attractions.

Some restaurants have a side room or other area that can be turned into a café for this purpose. The café room, or club room, can feature specialty coffee drinks, desserts and lighter foods. Music, cigars or even large screen televisions with appropriate videos, will all lend to a great atmosphere.

Whether you use an early bird, a night owl, or both, these time slots present another great opportunity to help out with the seating dilemma. If you are full during the rush hour, or if you simply want to move a group whose size does not fit into your seating plan, use the early and late experience as an alternative. Here is an example:

A group of eight wants to make a reservation for 7:30 p.m. You do not want to put a large party into the seating arrangement at that time. You could say, "I am sorry, we do not have a table open at that time", or you could use an incentive to MOVE that party into a better time slot.

Why not ask the guest a few questions to determine their willingness to move? For example:

"We are unable to seat you at that time. Is there some reason why your group needs to dine then? I am asking because we really would love to have you join us for dinner on Friday. If you would be willing to wait just one more hour, we can seat you at 8:30, and our manger would be pleased to serve you a bottle of complimentary champagne.

How much does a bottle of champagne cost? Not much compared to the profit from a party of eight. Will all groups switch to meet YOUR needs? No, but you can develop a program that will entice SOME of them to do it. And, don't forget to track the results, and reward the staff members who participate.

#10 The Chickens Don't Eat Dessert

Can we find a way to identify those people most likely to increase our contribution margin? Who will purchase an appetizer, dessert, or a bottle of wine? Do certain types of people order more? Does party size matter ?

The answers can only come from your guests' purchasing history. Observe your guests, record the information, then create sales TARGETS for your service staff.

Setting targets is a great way to increase sales, and at the same time, increase guest satisfaction. Remember, you cannot create strong demand without improving the satisfaction a guest receives from your restaurant. ANY time you uncover hidden money, you have overcome some frustration that was preventing your patrons from enjoying your restaurant to its fullest. There is just no other way it can happen!

Setting targets means you pick sales quotas for each server, under varying conditions. For example, you may determine that a party of six should order two bottles of wine on average. This information is given to the servers, who are told they will be evaluated on their ability to meet the goal. However, you don't simply tell them, "Sell two bottles of wine - or else." You TRAIN the staff in selling techniques, such as suggesting a red and a white wine for a mixed bag of entrée orders.

There are many other target goals to set. How many appetizers should a waiter sell per shift? What about desserts? And, don't forget the average check or contribution margin. A restaurant is a business, just like a car dealership. You wouldn't expect a car dealer to tell a salesperson, "This next customer is yours. If he buys a car, great. If not, you'll get another chance tomorrow." How long would that dealership stay in business?

Now, I am not suggesting that you train your people to use hardball selling tactics like those sometimes found in a car dealership. But, if you have customers who leave your restaurant without enjoying the *full extent of your service*, then they have not gotten their money's worth! And, if you have some servers who are not HELPING the guest by showing them the full range of possibilities, then both the guest, and your restaurant, are being short changed.

But, the servers will not <u>know</u> your expectations unless you tell them. Of course, you will <u>reward</u> them for achieving their goals. And, you will <u>rehabilitate</u> them if they do not - at least the first two times!

How do you set targets? First, gather information. Use a simple system to track the purchase habits of your guests. What does an average size party order? How many appetizers and how many desserts? Do men order more than women? And most importantly, do people who order certain entrees, such as a steak, order more desserts? It is easy to track. Simply make up a form and ask the servers (or assign a manager) to fill it out. Then, look over the results.

If a steak eater is more prone to order a dessert, for example, you can use this information to train the servers. And, you can use it to set standards. How many appetizers does a party of eight order? Look at your records. Then give the servers a target.

If the target is two (assuming the party will share them) and a server has a party that only orders one, the server can suggest a few additions, SELLING the party on the fun, the sharing, and the flavor! Servers can act with confidence, knowing the odds are on their side!

Does this require some work, and some expectations of server performance? Absolutely! But, you are the one who wanted to know where the money is hidden. You better go get it, otherwise, you may be selling cars!